My New

words by Josephine Croser
photographs by Nigel Croser

I have a new pet, and it needs a cage.

The cage is glass, so I can see in.

The cage has a lid, so my pet can't run away.

I put in some sawdust, so the cage can stay clean.

I put in a tube, so my pet can have a burrow. I put in some hay, so my pet can make a nest.

I put in some seeds and apple, so my pet can eat. I put in an old crust, so my pet can chew.

I put in a water bottle, so my pet can drink. I put in a ladder, so my pet can climb.

I put in a wheel, so my pet can run. I put in a box, so my pet can hide.

I put in my pet. It's a little mouse.
It sniffs around and hides.

Now it is running.

Look at it go!